Shepherding

Shepherding

STEPHEN KAUNG

CHRISTIAN FELLOWSHIP PUBLISHERS, INC.

NEW YORK

ISBN: 978-1-937713-37-9

Available from the Publishers at:

11515 Allecingie Parkway
Richmond, Virginia 23235
www.c-f-p.com

Printed in the United States of America

Foreword

Shepherding is one of the important functions in the church. It is not only one of the gifted people whom God gives to the church for the perfecting of the saints (see Ephesians 4:11-12 where pastors should be shepherds). It is also one of the main functions of the elders of the church (see I Peter 5:1). Indeed, it is expected of all the spiritual members of the church to be engaged in such a work. Our Lord's words to Peter were "feed my lambs," "shepherd my sheep," and "feed my sheep" (see John 21:15-17).

For this reason, it is required of us to know what the functions of shepherding are and also the qualifications. This series of three messages on shepherding is prepared for the promoting of God's work and the strengthening of this important but sadly lacking ministry in the church. May God use it for His glory.

TABLE OF CONTENTS

Unless otherwise indicated,
Scripture quotations are from the
New Translation by J. N. Darby.

Chapter 1

The Place of the Shepherd

> "I am the good shepherd. The good shepherd lays down his life for the sheep: but he who serves for wages, and who is not the shepherd, whose own the sheep are not, sees the wolf coming, and leaves the sheep and flees; and the wolf seizes them and scatters the sheep. Now he who serves for wages flees because he serves for wages, and is not himself concerned about the sheep. I am the good shepherd; and I know those that are mine, and am known of those that are mine, as the Father knows me and I know the Father; and I lay down my life for the sheep. And I have other sheep which are not of this fold: those also I must bring, and they shall hear my voice; and there shall be one flock, one shepherd" (John 10:11-16).

I was given the theme for this time and it is, "Pastoral Care in the Body of Christ." Now I dare not say that I am going to teach. But what I am trying to do is share with you dear brothers and sisters what the Lord has impressed upon my heart.

The more I meditate upon the theme, the more I am impressed with the importance of pastoral care in the body of Christ. In the past this matter of pastoral care was not as publicly recognized as it should have been. Only in recent years do we find that more and more this matter is being appreciated and recognized. Generally speaking, most of the people today appreciate teaching from the pulpit but not pastoral care. Teaching the word of God is more prominent and pastoral care is more hidden. Yet we find in the Scripture, pastor and teacher are one. In other words, teaching without pastoring will lose much of its effectiveness. It is the pastoral care that makes teaching more personal and also more experiential. I do believe that the Lord wants us to emphasize pastoring as much as teaching because these two are inseparable; they are one.

Poimen: "A Shepherd Tending the Flock"

This word, "pastor or shepherd" in the New Testament is from the Greek word *poimen* and it actually means "a shepherd tending the flock"; he is not only feeding them but really taking care of them in every way. This word is used in the Scripture especially in the New Testament. Firstly, it is used physically, which refers to those shepherds of the sheep, as we find in the Gospel of Luke, chapter 2. When our Lord Jesus came into this world, there were physical shepherds, shepherding ordinary sheep. Today, some people think that probably these shepherds were temple shepherds and were raising those sheep that were to be offered to God. It might very well be so, but either way we will find that first of all this word shepherd is used to apply to those physical shepherds of the sheep; that is one way of using that word.

Secondly, this word shepherd is used spiritually of our Lord Jesus. Our Lord Jesus is *the* Shepherd but not in a physical way of tending sheep in the wilderness. But in a spiritual way, He is shepherding His people. In the Gospel according to John, chapter 10, the Lord said, "I am the good Shepherd." Why is He a good Shepherd? It is because He laid down His life for His sheep. We cannot have a better Shepherd than the Lord himself who laid down His life for us.

The book of Hebrews chapter 13:20 tells us that He is the great Shepherd of the sheep. In the power of the blood of the eternal covenant, He is the great Shepherd. Why? Because through His blood He established a New Covenant, which is an eternal covenant made between God and us. In other words, everything that pertains to our spiritual life is in that New Covenant, and we have been brought into this through the blood of our Lord Jesus. No one can be greater than this; He is the great Shepherd.

It says in the first book of Peter chapter 5:4 that He is the Chief Shepherd. One day the Chief Shepherd shall be manifested and will reward those under-shepherds with a crown of everlasting glory. He is the Chief and all the other shepherds are under-shepherds. Thus this word, "Chief Shepherd" is applied to our Lord Jesus alone.

Thirdly, we will find this word "shepherd" in the New Testament is applied to certain people in the church which we find in the book of Ephesians chapter 4:11. After our Lord Jesus had ascended on high, He gave spiritual gifts to individuals and to the church—some apostles, some prophets, some evangelists, some pastors and teachers. Now the word "pastor" is the same Greek word *poimen*, which means shepherd. In some places it is translated in English as "shepherds"; but this is the only place where the same word is translated as "pastors." Probably it is just a matter of tradition, but this is the only time that this word "shepherd" is being translated into "pastor." In other words, pastor and shepherd are the same. This word is applied to God's people in verb form. In the book of Ephesians chapter 4:11, it is the only place in the New Testament that is in noun form. As a matter of fact, we find that pastors and teachers or shepherds and teachers are the same; they are not two different classes of people. God in His purpose gives four classes of people to the church for the perfecting of the saints—*some* apostles, *some* prophets, *some* evangelists and *some* pastors (or shepherds) and teachers.[1] For this reason, we can distinguish that pastors and teachers are actually one class of people with different titles. Teachers are normally more in the sense of public work and pastors' work are more hidden and personal, but actually both are serving in the same area.

Fourthly, we will find this word in verb form used twice in the New Testament. One is in the book of Acts chapter 20 where the apostle Paul in his farewell speech

---

[1] The word "some" is only used four times in this passage, once before each class of worker. The terms "pastor" and "teacher" are combined here into one class.

to the elders in the church at Ephesus was telling them that God had sent the Holy Spirit to set them as overseers over the assembly of God. They were to shepherd the flock of God, which He had purchased with the blood of His own Son. Those elders of the church in Ephesus were to shepherd the flock of God; that is their function (see v. 28).

Also again, this is mentioned in the first book of Peter chapter 5:l-2. Here Peter was writing to his fellow elders and witnesses of the suffering of the Lord and there he said, "You, whom God has chosen, you are to shepherd the flock, exercising and overseeing the flock of God." Actually it means being "shepherders"—taking upon yourselves the character of a shepherd in your relationship with the flock of God.

Brothers and sisters, so far as this word shepherd is concerned in the Bible, if it is not applied to the physical, which is the literal shepherd, then it either applies to our Lord Jesus as *the* Shepherd or it may apply to two different classes of people in the church. One is shepherds or pastors and teachers as one class of people that God has given to the church for the perfecting of the saints. They are in the area of "the work of God." We can call them "workers." These men are called by God to perfect the saints. Therefore, in this area of the work of God, we will find the titles of shepherds, pastors and teachers. And the other class of people is in the area of the church itself, in which God has put this shepherding care upon the elders of the church. In the New Testament these two classes of people are to be shepherds of the flock of God. One class belongs to the "work" (Ephesians 4); the other class belongs to the "church" (I Peter 5), and these are to do the work of shepherding the flock of God.

Strangely, we will find the Scripture mentions "Philip the evangelist," but nowhere in the New Testament does it mention Timothy as the "pastor" or Apollos as the "teacher". But we find today we have so many with the title "pastor" or "teacher." Oftentimes, we realize that when the Scripture is silent, men are most vocal. So here we find "pastor" is either a person as pastor or teacher (see Eph. 4), or a function as elders in the church (see 1 Peter 5). The main function of the elders is pastoral care. It should never be a title, but unfortunately, today among God's people it is more of a title than a function. This does not mean that in the Scripture "pastoral care" is being done officially, if we may use it in this way. Officially, the pastors and teachers in the work of God, and the elders in the church all exercise pastoral care; but that does not mean that it is limited just to these groups of people.

Pastoral Care, a Function for All

As a matter of fact, pastoral care is a function for all the members of the body of Christ. And being members one of another in the body of Christ involves a certain measure of pastoral care. In other words, how can one member not care for another member? If we are in the body of Christ, there is no way for us not to care for one another. It is something built within us after we are saved. We have to bear one another's burdens. We have to care for one another. We have to be concerned for one another because in doing so we are caring for ourselves. We belong to the same body—the strong taking care of the weak and the grown-up taking care of the young. The more mature and more spiritual are to take care of the less spiritual. Every brother and sister has a responsibility in a smaller or larger degree in this area of pastoral care or shepherding.

In the book of Galatians, chapter 6, we are told, "If anyone among you is at fault, those who are spiritual are to restore them in the spirit of meekness." We can put it in another way, if a person is more spiritual he is to take care of the less spiritual. Then immediately following it says, "We have to bear one another's burden, thus to fulfill the law of God, the law of Christ." It is the law of love. Evidently, in the body we will find that the law is love. If the law is love, how can we not be concerned with one another? How can we not bear one another's burden? Should we not do so? Therefore, in a very general way, we may say that every brother and every sister is and should be involved in this matter of pastoral care in the body of Christ. If we leave the pastoral care just to pastors and teachers and elders, they will be utterly exhausted and unable to fulfill the responsibility. This is the area of the function of the church that we need to emphasize. It is true, God does give to the church some shepherds and teachers; this is their work, their commission and they should do it, and do it faithfully. Surely, it is true that those elders in the church are supposed to take care of the flock; this is their responsibility and they should do it. But it does not mean that because they are doing the pastoral care, hence all the rest of the people do not need to do anything. This is really a great weakness in the church today.

We thank God for those pastors and teachers. The church needs such ones. We are grateful for the elders who faithfully shepherd the flock, but if we really understand the heart of God, I believe that everyone should bear some measure of pastoral care in the body of Christ. If pastoral care functions the way it should, then we will find the body can really grow in a healthy way. It is a good thing, especially for someone who is spiritually more advanced in the Lord, who has established experiential knowledge of the Lord. Even if we do not hold any official position in the church, it is a great asset for all of those who are a little bit more mature spiritually in the Lord to bear, care and love one or two brothers or sisters in their hearts. Everyone should have someone upon their heart. This is similar to how we encourage every believer to have a burden in his or her heart for the salvation of one or two unbelievers. They should bear these people in their hearts, pray for them and pursue them until they come to the Lord. This is evangelism. Every brother and sister should pray for at least one or two unsaved persons, and maybe one will be able to have more in their heart to see them through to be saved. After these people, whom we are praying for their salvation are saved, immediately we should take up another one, and this is the way to fulfill the gospel being preached. It is the same way in the body of Christ regarding pastoral care. Therefore, in the body of Christ we should encourage brothers and sisters to be before the Lord to have at least one upon his or her heart and really pray for that person's spiritual well-being. When that person is absent from a meeting, we call, we pursue, and we bear that particular one in our heart. And by doing so we will see that not only will that person be greatly helped spiritually, but we ourselves will be greatly strengthened as well. This is the essential way that pastoral care should be taken up in the church of God.

We do not want to limit pastoral care to just these two classes of people. We appreciate them, but we find that they alone are not able to take care of the whole flock of God. Truly in the house of God we need to encourage brothers and sisters to enter in and participate in this essential function.

Why Pastoral Care is so Essential

Why is pastoral care so essential in the body of Christ? It is very obvious for us to see why, because the Bible calls believers sheep which is an excellent term. When we think of sheep—innocent, pure, meek—everybody loves them, but that is only one side of it. There is the other side. Among all the domesticated animals there are none dumber or more ignorant than sheep. According to the Bible, God's people are like sheep. Sometimes we think of God's people partially in a good way, and we should, for they are so lovely, ignorant, and innocent. That is why we often hear that all the trouble in the church is with the leaders, for the people are sheep and they are no problem, except that is only one side to consider.

There is the other side; sheep are normally dumb and ignorant. They cannot distinguish between the nutritious and the poisonous. That is the reason why sheep need a shepherd, because if we just let the sheep go their own way they will eat anything. They do not know that this particular grass or herb is poisonous or whether it is good for them; again they just cannot distinguish between them. Unfortunately, that is what we often find among God's children. The more we are among them the more we realize how ignorant they are. Sometimes we feel like we want to give up on them. We think they should be mature by now, but they are not. So in this case, do we blame them? In reality that is what they are; they are sheep. How essential it is for them to have shepherds! They need someone who can help them find good pastures, keep them from the poisonous grass and enable them to find that which is nutritious. How much do sheep need shepherding! We cannot just let them go their own way because they are ignorant, and once they get lost they will be unable to find their way back. They do not have the horses' sense who can find their way back when they are lost. But if sheep get lost we have to go after them and find them. Sheep will not be able to find their way back and that is why they need shepherds. We realize that God's people are as sheep. If they get lost we cannot wait until they come back by themselves; they are unlikely to return, so we will have to go and find them. Not only that, sheep are defenseless. If they accidently are trapped in a thorn bush, they are not able to get themselves out. They are also absolutely defenseless before the wolves, bears or lions. They are among the most defenseless animals. For example, goats have horns to defend themselves but sheep have none. Therefore, they need to be protected. If we really understand the sheep, it almost seems as if the shepherd will have to take care of everything for them. We have already mentioned God's people are like sheep. This is who we are dealing with and who we are taking care of. Oftentimes we expect too much of our brothers and sisters; this causes us to be discouraged and blame them for not being able to grow in the way we expect them to. For this reason, we who are shepherding the flock need to have an understanding of the sheep. That is the reality of who we are dealing with—God's people who are like sheep. They are so lovely and yet we have to take care of them in all aspects. Thus, that is why pastoral care in the body of Christ is so essential.

Among God's people we find that there are extremes. We are all naturally extremists. Do not think we are balanced until the Lord balances us. On the one hand, some people go to one extreme and say, "Well, I do not need anybody or any pastoral care; just the Lord and I. That's enough." It seems as if they do not belong to the flock of God. They are the "flock"; one sheep. That is one extreme. On the other hand, we will find another group of people who go to the other extreme and say, "Well, because God's people are sheep, they need to be taken care of. Therefore, let us organize, plan, and arrange a system." So it becomes artificially done. We then arrange some people to be their shepherds and put them under a so-called "super-shepherd" as a hierarchy system. Afterwards we will find these shepherds begin to feel, "Well, the sheep are dumb, the sheep are ignorant, and they cannot do anything. All they need to do is listen to me." So they will do everything for them. These are some extremes and we need to strike the balance.

In one way we do see the need of pastoral care in the body of Christ; it is a tremendous need. We pray that God will raise up many, many people who are able to function in this way because much teaching on shepherding is lost. We realize some people appreciate teaching—ones who stand before the pulpit to teach—however, their teaching is one thing, but without the accompanying of pastoral care most of the teaching will be ineffective. So we do see the need of pastoral care in the body of Christ. At the same time we need to be very careful lest we fall into the other extreme—making it a human institution. In that way, we institutionalize the shepherding or the pastoring.

One Flock, One Shepherd

One principle in the Scripture that we need to understand concerning this matter of pastoral care in the body of Christ is very basic. We can read from the Gospel according to John chapter 10:16 that the Lord says, "One flock, one shepherd." That is the basic principle of pastoral care in the body of Christ. There is only one flock. The Lord said, "There are some sheep not in this fold." Of course, when He was speaking, He referred to Judaism as a religion. Judaism is like a fold and there are people in it and the Lord gets some sheep out from that fold. The Lord said, "Yet, there are other sheep that are not in this fold; I have to find them." The Lord was indicating Gentiles and they are in another fold, and He will take some out from among them. God will bring these into one flock as His own—many folds but only one flock. At the time, when the Lord was on the earth, there were only two folds—Judaism and heathenism. But today we have many more folds, but remember there is only one flock of the Lord. Why is it so? Because we find it so easy to consider those who are under our care as our own flock. I often hear people say, "My flock." Now I may ask: Whose flock is it? theirs or the Lord's? For these sheep do not belong to anyone else; they belong to the Lord alone. The Lord has purchased them with His own precious blood; this flock is His property and His possession.

In the first book of Peter chapter 5 we find the exhortation of Peter to these elders who are to shepherd the flock: "Now do not think that they are your private possession. Do not lord over them as if they are your private possession." No, they are the Lord's property. We need to recognize that all the sheep belong to the Lord and all His sheep are in one flock; there are not many flocks. Unfortunately, the world may have many folds, but there is only one flock of God. This shows us that we who are the Lord's are one; we cannot be divided. The oneness of the body of Christ is again expressed in the one flock and this is a basic understanding. God may give us the burden to take care of them but never look at them as if they belong to us as our personal, private property.

"One flock and one shepherd" (see John 10:16). How many shepherds are there? There is actually only one Shepherd, and this one Shepherd is none other than the Lord himself. In other words, God does give to the church some shepherds, some pastors and also raises up elders to shepherd the flock. At the same time, God burdens us for caring for one another; yet we have to remember that in spite of all this there is only one Shepherd. How can that be? It simply means when we are shepherding, it is not we who are shepherding, but it is *the* Shepherd, the Lord himself, who is shepherding within us and through us. Let's put it in another way: there is no one who can shepherd anybody, because souls are too precious to the Lord to be committed to anybody. We would like to emphasize that souls are so precious that God will never commit any soul to anyone besides himself, lest we destroy that soul. For He has paid such a great price for that soul and has such hope for that person. He has destined that soul to such glory far beyond what we can imagine. Do we think He will commit His redeemed one to anybody else? No. One Shepherd and one only. It is true that He does use His people in this work of shepherding, but we must always remember when we are shepherding, it is not we who are doing it but the Lord himself. And if we remember this, it will keep us away from all of those errors, mistakes, and tragedies that are happening in the church today. Therefore, we dare not do anything on our own, for we have to ask the Lord to enlighten us to see if it is the Lord who is doing the shepherding. This principle is basic but must be kept. In other words, it is not only in the matter of shepherding, it is also in the matter of teaching or anything that is related to the work of God. Anything that is concerned with spiritual responsibilities or with the redeemed ones, we find God reserves the right for himself. Yet because of this, brother and sisters, how much we need the working of the cross in our lives.

The tragedy in shepherding is that we begin to think that the flock is ours and we begin to shepherd them according to our own thoughts. We may think it is the best, but it is from ourselves and it is imperfect. How we need to do the work of shepherding with fear and trembling! How much we need the cross to work in our lives that we dare not touch anybody with our soulish hands! Brothers and sisters, when the Lord, the Chief Shepherd is able to shepherd through us, then we find that the sheep are blessed. One flock, one Shepherd—this is the basic principle in the pastoral care in the body of Christ.

Relationship

Of course, in this matter of shepherding one thing is very important and that is relationship. There must be a relationship developed between the shepherd and the sheep. Between the one who is pastoring and the one receiving the care, it is essential to establish this relationship. In the Gospel according to John, chapter 10, the Lord said: "I am the Shepherd and I know my sheep by name." Here we are not talking about an outward or superficial relationship but a real relationship, because the Lord knows every sheep by name. Name here does not mean just any name; it means an identification. In other words, the Lord knows His sheep.

When we read the Bible, we find that the names used in the Bible are really wonderful and meaningful. For instance, the name Jacob represents his character. We remember the Bible uses the name Jacob in the beginning (which means "supplanter"), but then he was transformed into Israel (which means "prince of God" or "wrestler"). This name Israel is a new identification because he became a new person in the Lord. Names are very meaningful and wonderful in the Bible. Unfortunately, today we find that names hardly mean anything at all. They do not have any meaning to any particular person, neither do they identify people as in the old days. For example, a child was given a name because of the expectation of the parents for that child. Or something is seen by the parents in that child that reminds them of a certain name. Or a name is given when the grace of God came upon that person and transformed him.

Name is an identification and the Lord knows every sheep by name. If He has a hundred sheep, He has a hundred names for a hundred sheep. He has a name for every one of us. It may not be the name we had originally, but He has a name for each one of us, and that name really identifies us; whereas our names today do not identify us. But the Lord calls us by name and that name identifies us. He knows exactly who we are, where we are, and He knows exactly what His grace can bring us to, what He can accomplish in us, and how He can be glorified in us. Our Lord knows everything. Therefore, anyone who is going to be involved in some measure of pastoral care, the first thing to do is to establish a relationship between himself and the sheep. And if we do not have this relationship established we are not able to counsel anyone. We know that some people have pet doctrines in counseling, and they use the same formula for whoever comes; it is like giving the same medicine and expecting it to cure all diseases. But unfortunately, it does not work that way in spiritual counseling, for everyone we deal with is different. Every sheep is different and we ought to know each one before we are able to really help them. Otherwise, our help will become superficial because we do not know them and their real problems. So first of all, we will find that whoever is doing this pastoral care has to know the sheep by name and be able to identify with this person. Surely, it will take time to accomplish the task because it is a long process; but we have to do it.

In the book of Proverbs chapter 27 it says, "Be well acquainted with the appearance of the flock; look well to thy herds" (v. 23). A relationship has to be established and then out of the relationship comes trust. We cannot care for anyone who does not trust us, neither can we care for anyone whom we do not trust. And needless to say, if we have already given up on that particular person we will no longer be able to take care of him because we assume he is good for nothing and will never be improved. Therefore, there must be a mutual trust and this trust is built up gradually between the two parties.

Remember David in Psalm 23: "The Lord is my Shepherd." Now we are all familiar with the "The Lord is my Shepherd, I shall not want," but when David said, "the Lord is my Shepherd," he meant, "I put myself under His care, I trust Him." Again, if a sheep does not trust the shepherd, he cannot do anything for this particular one; he will not listen to the voice of the shepherd; he will go his own way. We know how important this is. Out of establishing this relationship will result in a trust for one another. Because a mutual trust has to be there for pastoral care to be effective.

Moses, a Shepherd-King

When we think of pastoral care, Moses is the one person in the Old Testament who stands out the most. For the first forty years of Moses' life he was brought up in the palace in Egypt where he was trained to be a king. And by the training he received, he became qualified to be the king of Egypt; but somehow he felt compassion in his heart for his own brethren. Perhaps the seed to save Israel was planted in him while his mother was nursing him. He felt a calling towards his brethren. He was concerned about their welfare, so when he was forty years of age, he went out and looked on their sufferings. We are all familiar with the story of how he killed an Egyptian, and then the next day he went out again and tried to make peace between two Hebrews who were quarreling with each other, for he was "mighty in words and in deeds." That was the way he had been trained in Egypt to become a king; but that was not the purpose of God for Moses. To be able to rule over Egypt was his natural ability, but that did not qualify him to shepherd God's people. As a result, God took him to the wilderness for forty years where he tended sheep. Sometimes we wonder why God allowed this to happen. The reason is because God's idea for Moses was for him to be a "shepherd-king", or "king-shepherd." For the first forty years Moses was trained to be a king in Egypt and not a shepherd. His hand was too heavy on other people; he was too eloquent in his speech; and he was too confident in himself. So God took him away for another forty years in the wilderness to tend sheep.

During these forty years God developed in him a shepherd's heart. He learned a lot during those forty years—he learned who God is, he learned about himself, and he learned to know the sheep. At the time he was in Egypt, he neither knew God nor himself nor the children of Israel. He thought at the time that the children of Israel surely appreciated his help. It seemed that they should have known he was there to help them, but they did not. The reason was that the children of Israel were sheep—dumb with a lack of understanding—neither did he know himself nor did he know the way of God. So in that second forty years of Moses' life God allowed him to go through his most humbling and humiliating experience until his eloquence and his might were gone. He was no longer confident in himself, but he began to know God, he began to know himself, and he began to know the sheep. Afterward God sent him back to Egypt to deliver the children of Israel which began the third forty year period of his life.

The books of Exodus, Numbers, and Deuteronomy tell us how Moses had been trained by God as a shepherd-king. On one hand, he was among the most capable of people, but on the other hand, we will find that a shepherd's heart was in him, and this showed forth again and again. We recall that he led the Israelites to Mount Sinai and he went up the mountain to receive the Ten Commandments from God. While the children of Israel were waiting for Moses to come down from the mountain, because of his delay they were wondering why it took Moses so long and were afraid that he was not coming back, so they made a golden calf (see Exodus 31:1). They made a golden calf and worshiped it; they broke the law of God. When Moses came down from Mount Sinai and saw that the people had gone astray so quickly, he had to deal quite drastically with them. He burned the golden calf, ground it to powder, scattered it upon the water and made the children of Israel drink it. In other words, they had to drink their own sin. Then he called for those who were on the Lord's side; he stood at the gate of the camp because the camp was polluted, and called: "Who is on the Lord's side?" And all the sons of Levi came to Moses. Even though they were just as sinful as their brethren, but they repented and joined Moses. The result was that they had to go into the camp and slay everyone they met on the way whoever that one might be—whether it be his brother or his neighbor. This great sin was drastically dealt with (see Exodus 32:1-10, 15-29).

Afterwards Moses went to God and there he pleaded with Him: "Forgive them; if You do not, blot me out of Thy book that You have written" (see Exodus 32:32). Now that is a shepherd's heart. Moses was very firm before the people because he stood for God's purpose. At the same time he was so humble and lowly before God because he identified himself with the sheep—with the people. This is a true character needed for shepherding. Then we will find again and again this special pastoral character continued to play out in Moses' life.

In the book of Numbers, chapter 11, after the people left Mount Sinai, they began to journey towards the Promised Land. And they continued to tempt the Lord ten times; they refused to believe in the Lord because they did not trust Him. For they were afraid of giants and did not want to go into the Promised Land; instead, they wanted to go back to Egypt. At that time God said to Moses: "I will destroy this people and make you a great nation." But Moses pleaded with God and said, "This is Your people. You have brought them out with a mighty hand, and everybody knows about it. If You destroy them now, people will say it is because You are not able to bring them into the land flowing with milk and honey. Where then will be Your honor?" And God listened to Moses.

When we look at the children of Israel we see that they are but sheep—stubborn, no understanding, rebellious—and for even little things they rebelled and blamed Moses. They murmured against him and wanted to stone him because they had forgotten what he had done for them. If God was provoked by the children of Israel, certainly Moses was even more so. But God said to him, "Take them in your arms; carry them," but Moses said, "I was not the one who brought them out from Egypt." However, God said, "Carry them in your arms." So Moses did. He was the meekest of all men.

Now brothers and sisters, this is an example of pastoral care in the body of Christ. Do not think that pastoral care is something glorious. It is easy to give birth to a new believer who needs pastoral care, but to bring that soul to maturity in the Lord is the hardest thing to do. But thank God, because the Lord is the Chief Shepherd. He shares His heart with His own people and wants His people to join with Him in the responsibility of shepherding care. One important thing we need to remember—one flock, one Shepherd.

Dear Heavenly Father, we do praise and thank You because You do show us that Your Son, our Lord Jesus, is the Shepherd, the good Shepherd, the great Shepherd, the Chief Shepherd. Lord, we do thank You that You have put these burdens upon Your people in the body of Christ to join with You to be vessels in Your hand for this pastoring care, because You do care for Your sheep. Oh Father, we ask that You will give us a shepherd's heart. We pray that Christ the Shepherd may so fill us to enable us to do this work of shepherding among Your people. Lord, do not allow us to be so bold as to think we can do it, but we pray that we may give ourselves to You, not for our sake but for Yours. Lord, we are willing to be used by You in this way. Oh, raise up more brothers and sisters who are able to care for Your people. Your people are like sheep without shepherds—scattered and harassed. Oh Lord, Your heart must be groaning and crying out. Do let us hear Your cry. Lord, even though this is a most unappreciative and hard function, yet if it is Your will and if it pleases You, we are willing to follow Your footsteps.

So here we just offer ourselves to You and pray that we will consider it a great honor if You should put this burden upon us. But Lord, do not allow us to be presumptuous; keep us very humble before You. Lord, who is competent to do this? Our competency comes from You. So we just commit ourselves and commit this whole matter of pastoral care in the body of Christ into Your hands and pray that in this very short time that we are together You will bring us into the understanding of pastoral care, that Your body may be built up to the praise of Your Glory. In the name of our Lord Jesus. Amen.

Chapter 2

The Work of the Shepherd

Psalm 23:1-6—"Jehovah is my shepherd; I shall not want. He maketh me to lie down in green pastures; he leadeth me beside still waters. He restoreth my soul; he leadeth me in paths of righteousness for his name's sake. Yea, though I walk through the valley of the shadow of death, I will fear no evil: for thou art with me; thy rod and thy staff, they comfort me. Thou prepares a table before me in the presence of mine enemies; thou hast anointed my head with oil; my cup runneth over. Surely, goodness and loving-kindness shall follow me all the days of my life; and I will dwell in the house of Jehovah for the length of the days."

This is a Psalm written by David, the shepherd-king. Because he was a shepherd, he knew his sheep, and at the same time, being a sheep himself, he knew God as his Shepherd. I think probably no one in the world appreciates the Lord as the Shepherd more than David did. Not only because of his experience with sheep but more so because of his personal experience with the Lord as his Shepherd. Out of his experience of the Lord he composed this beautiful Psalm. It is not just a beautiful Psalm, it is real; it is living.

"The Lord Is My Shepherd"

He begins with, "The Lord is my Shepherd, I shall not want." It is because he himself is a sheep and he recognizes what he is; thus he is very thankful that he knows *the* Shepherd. And he committed himself totally to that One and that is the reason why he says, "The Lord is my Shepherd." Nowadays, there are sheep who do not recognize themselves, who think they are wise, they are clever, they are able, and they are sufficient in themselves; thus they think they do not need a shepherd, so they wander away from the flock. They go their own way and if the shepherd does not go out to find them, they end up in disaster. But there are also sheep who are conscious of their own weaknesses, who recognize they are not self-sufficient and realize the need of a shepherd. They are willing to put themselves under the care of the Lord through those shepherds. These are the blessed ones.

"I Shall Not Want"

We whom are sharing the part of shepherding care need to have a total commitment of ourselves to the Lord, and if we commit ourselves to Him, we find that He is totally committed to us. If we are in this condition we can say, "I shall not want." Normally, we all have wants of many kinds and different sorts of things; but if we really commit ourselves to the Lord as our Shepherd, then we no longer have our wants but all our needs are being met by Him. It may not be met in the way we expected, nonetheless, we will find that our needs are always met because the Lord is our Shepherd.

In this matter of pastoral care, I think no one is qualified to be involved if he or she has not experienced the pastoring care of the Lord in their personal life. In engaging in the work of shepherding we ourselves must learn the lesson and the experience of being shepherded by the Lord. We cannot take care of anybody spiritually more than what we have been taken care of by the Lord. It is because in this matter of shepherding, it is not just a matter of giving out some counseling, some principles, or some teachings; it is actually sharing Christ with one another. Because we were in need and in want before, consequently, we found that our Lord Jesus, being our Shepherd, has supplied our every need. Because of that, out of such experience we are able to help our brothers and sisters. It will not be our head-knowledge or second-hand information, nor some skills or formulas that we have learned previously that will equip us to shepherd people. It has to come from our own experience of the Lord himself as our Shepherd that can really help them.

In this Psalm 23 we are going to emphasize in David's life how he found the Lord as his Shepherd. I think it would be a very profitable study if we meditate on this Psalm with the life of David in view before us, because whatever he says in this Psalm is his experience of the Lord as his Shepherd. It is not a theory to him; so we can apply every word in this Psalm to understand some phases of David's life and how he experienced the Lord as his Shepherd. Or to put it another way, he found the Lord as his all and in all. It would be a very profitable study or meditation to do this, but we would like to walk through this Psalm a little bit differently. Here David is telling us of what the good, the great, the Chief Shepherd has done in his life, touching and covering many areas of his life. And we would like to use this to show what the different things are that a shepherd does. When we are doing shepherding or pastoral care, what are the qualifications that are expected of us? What should we do? What is included in this pastoral care? That is something we would like to share together before the Lord; because after all, not only all pastoral care in the church is patterned after the Lord's, but more than that, we need to know that He who is shepherding is shepherding through us.

Knowing Christ as the Green Pasture

First of all he said, "He maketh me to lie down in green pastures." We have already mentioned that the sheep have no knowledge of the different kinds of pastures. They do not know how to distinguish between a good pasture and a bad one. They are not able to distinguish between the nutritious and the poisonous ones. The sheep are totally ignorant of the knowledge of them; it is the shepherds who find the pastures for the sheep. The shepherds know where the green pastures are. The pastures are not to be barren, withered, and scorched; instead they are to be green, fresh, living, and nutritious. The shepherds know their sheep so well and know that at a certain time the sheep need certain kinds of herbs; so they will lead them to the suitable pasture. Good shepherds will lead sometimes to a certain pasture and at other times to another pasture because they know there are different needs as the sheep grow; it is not just one kind of green pasture but many different kinds of pastures. Because the shepherds know the needs of their sheep—their various needs at various times, at various stages of growth—therefore, they will choose the suitable pastures for them. They will let them feed upon the green pastures to the extent that they are so well-fed that after they have eaten so much they are able to lie down in green pastures. In other words, there is such an abundance of these grasses that after they have eaten, the pastures still remain green and the shepherds will make them lie down. It does not mean that they force them to lie down; it simply means that they are so satisfied that they will lie down and chew what they have eaten, and that becomes nutrition for their body. That is what the shepherds should do.

If we apply this spiritually, what are the green pastures? Of course, we know this indicates the Lord Jesus himself; He is our pasture. He is not only our Shepherd; He is also our green pastures which speaks of the unsearchable riches of Christ. He offers His riches to us and leads us to himself. It is never something old nor something traditional, but it is always living, fresh, and green; that is what our Lord Jesus is.

We who are involved in this shepherding must find green pastures for the flock of God. Imagine without doing so that the outcome will be the poverty, hunger, and undernourishment of God's people as we see today. It is very true that we find God's people hungering and thirsting spiritually. This is not for their physical need—water and food, as it were—they are hungering and thirsting for the word of God. The word of God is the living word; Christ is the living Word of God. For the word of God is not just doctrines, as teachings, as traditional concepts, but the word of God should be fresh and living through the power of the Holy Spirit. And if it is a reality in our lives then we will be able to experience Christ in the word. It is not just the written word, but by the power of the Holy Spirit it has become living and is green pastures to us. In other words, we ourselves experience the Lord as the green pastures. Because we personally know the unsearchable riches of Christ, therefore we are able to lead the flock to these pastures. That is the reason why we can never shepherd or care for our dear brothers and sisters more than what we actually know or experience of the Lord.

Oftentimes we think of shepherding or pastoring as an external work. If we have some head knowledge of the word of God, or if we collect or memorize some Scriptures from the Bible and assume we know all the word of God, then we assume we know the way of God. Or maybe we have learned some knowledge of how to shepherd from school, from books or from some people and if we begin to shepherd others assuming we know the way to do so, we will lead them to old, barren, scorched, and withered pastures. No wonder we find God's people are so hungry today.

It amazes me that sometimes people can be Christians for ten or fifteen years and regularly meet in a certain place, yet not be able to bear any fruit. Today we see all kinds of liberal churches and so-called fundamental churches where these Christians have been going to church meetings for so many years. But when they come to the word of God we find they do not know much of anything because they have been led to one pasture all the time which means they emphasize one doctrine instead of the whole counsel of God. They have only been fed upon a certain pasture; but as they grow they need other pastures of different kinds of nutrition. No wonder these Christians do not grow and remain in the same condition for years and years. The reason is because those who are pastoring them, who are shepherding them, do not know any better themselves. Thus, how important it is to be burdened to function in the Lord's way in this matter of shepherding in the body of Christ.

We ourselves need to know Christ as the green pasture in a personal way. For He is not just milk which is predigested food, but we need to know the Lord as solid food. Christ is the green pasture and we as sheep are fed and satisfied, then we are able to lie down and chew the cud, and let the nutrition of the food really become part of us. Sometimes we hear someone teaching about certain things and immediately we will say to ourselves: "Well, now I have it." Then we go out and teach other people even before we have digested it. I am not saying that we cannot take what we have heard and pass it on to other people. We realize that no one is the originator of the word except the Lord himself. Even the words preached by the apostles were not original because they were all given by God. So if people think they are the originator, something is wrong and it must be a strange doctrine made up by themselves. To pass on what we have heard or what we have read is perfectly all right, but always remember, we cannot do the "pass on process" before we ourselves have really digested it. When we have digested the food, laid down in green pastures and are satisfied it is as if we are enlightened by the Lord in a certain aspect of His word through chewing and digesting it, and it is no longer secondhand knowledge but it becomes personal as *rhema*[2]. Afterwards, it is perfectly all right for us to share with one another what we have heard. The reason why the Lord has fed us in this way is not for ourselves alone but through us to feed other brothers and sisters. So we who are doing this pastoral care must know the Lord as the green pasture to equip us for this function.

Inasmuch as we know the Lord in this way then we can lie down and rest. The Lord has made us lie down in green pastures in order to help our fellow believers in the same way. The main goal of the Lord is not for His sheep

---

[2] Here the use of the Greek word *rhema* for "word" is used to emphasize the experience of the word verses the fact of the word *logos*.

to taste of himself partially here and there, but He wants us to help them in a consistent way and share with them the immense riches of the Lord so that they are able to lie down and chew the cud which will become very nutritious to them.

The problem today is that we have a tendency to say to those who are newly saved, "All right, we will put you to work." We do not give them time to lie down, but we request of them to work right away, keeping them busy and involved in "so-called Christian works." I am afraid this is the way that Christianity has been doing and is still doing today. Since that is the case, what will be the result? The result will be starving Christians trying to feed other Christians who are equally or more starved than themselves. No wonder these starving Christians have no rest. We put them to work as if work is more important than their communion with the Lord. We think being actively involved is more important than being quiet before Him. At the end of it will be a disastrous result for they are not ready to serve.

In this matter of pastoral care, when we see our brothers and sisters, the first thing we need to do is to lead them to Christ so that they can feed upon the Lord and are therefore able to really rest in the Lord. Now rest does not mean that they just go to sleep; rest means that they ruminate over the word that they heard; they chew the cud and digest it. Never rush them into service. Oftentimes, we see a person who is newly saved and he seems to be quite zealous for the Lord. And when we see such a Christian, immediately we say to the person: "Do this and do that; take care of something; run here and there." We put him to work before he even has time to digest what he has received of God's word.

In pastoral care the first thing we need to do is to lead the sheep to lie down in green pastures. Have we done that? Is this what we are doing? Are we failing in this aspect? Most likely, the reason why the church in general has failed is because we ourselves have failed in the same manner; for we do not know any better. The reason our knowledge of the Lord is so meager is because we only know Him as our Savior. But thank God, we know that He is not only our Savior and has forgiven our sins, but we also have eternal life. In the beginning we did not even know what "eternal life" was. We assumed that it is like a life insurance policy and will become effective after we die, but it is of no value while we are still alive. Now if that is the mentality we have, then how can we expect more out of the people whom we are taking care of? First of all, the most fundamental and elementary thing of pastoral care is to lead the sheep to lie down in green pastures, and that is what David experienced of the Lord. Because he experienced the Lord in this way, thus he was able to shepherd the nation of Israel in the same way and bring them into the riches of Christ.

Know the Indwelt Holy Spirit

The second point is: "He leads me beside still waters." From this verse we can see that drinking is just as important as eating. As a matter of fact, we can fast for a number of days but without drinking any water for a number of days, we will not be able to live. We know how important it is to drink water, because water will not only quench our thirst, it will help digest the food we eat. It will also provide nutrition to our whole body and purify our system. We realize how essential and important water is in our daily lives.

After the sheep have fed on the green pastures and are chewing the cud, the next thing that the shepherd will do is lead them beside the still waters. "He leadeth me beside still waters"; it provides drink for them. We are told that the sheep dare not drink any water that is rushing in a torrent, because they are afraid they will be drowned. Therefore, we have to lead them to still waters in order for them to drink, which will help them digest the food they have eaten and give the necessity to sustain their bodies. It is a good and essential process they need.

So what are these "still waters"? Spiritually speaking, still waters represent the Holy Spirit. He is the river of the water of life. When the Holy Spirit speaks, He speaks with a still small voice; it is as the still water. He does not come in an overwhelming, rushing, forcing way; He comes in such gentleness and stillness but so persistently and constantly. That is the difference between the work of the enemy, the devil and the work of the Holy Spirit. If it comes from the enemy, it will come overwhelmingly upon us and try to wipe us out. But when it comes from the Holy Spirit, it is so gentle, soft, kind, and yet so persistent. It is like an anointing within us. Suppose we have a wound that needs some ointment which will give a very soothing feeling and heal the wound. That is the way the Holy Spirit works.

In our discussion on pastoral care, we have said that we usually lead people to ourselves. For instance, when we are shepherding people, we often lead them to ourselves, we give them advice, show them the way, and tell them what they ought to do. In one sense, it is simple not only to them but to us also; because it seems like we are supposed to be in a knowledgeable position. We know what to do but they do not. Because of this, the easy thing for us to do is just tell them or teach them. It is not only an easy way out for us, it is also easy for them to get the answer so they do not need to pray. They do not need to seek the Lord or wait on the Holy Spirit and let Him speak to them because we have already told them what to do. In pastoral care our greatest temptation is to substitute ourselves for the Holy Spirit. We act as God. It is one of the greatest temptations if we are not careful in this aspect of shepherding. In a sense, that is the quick and easy way to solve problems for them and for us. Now if we know the answer or the direction for them, how we need to restrain ourselves from telling them right away what to do, even though it is very difficult for us to do that. We know by saying just one word to a person who is seeking us for guidance from the Lord, the problem will be solved immediately; yet we have to hold back and let that person go through the agony of waiting upon the Lord. We have to allow the Spirit of God to tell this person what to do. It seems as if we are not trying to help them; but we are making it more difficult for that person when we try to tell them what they ought to do. Unfortunately, out of our good heart and good intention, we will make a quick fix. In doing so, we may solve his problem quickly for the moment, but that person will not learn the lesson himself. He will be unable to know how to go to the Lord or listen to the voice of the Holy Spirit. He will have no direct communion with the Lord nor have understanding of the way of the Lord. He will fully depend upon us instead of the Lord. His whole Christian life will be an external way; there is no internal relationship with God. His whole Christian life is spoiled and it is because of our good intention of trying to help him have an easy way out. Therefore, if a brother or sister comes to you with a problem and if you know the solution right away, please do not give advice too quickly. Instead, try to lead them to the still waters. Let him drink of the Spirit just as the psalmist says of the hart which loves the water-brook (see Psalm 42:1). Do we know why? Because the water-brook not only quenches the thirst of the hart but it can look at the water-brook and see its own reflection. So we can use it in a spiritual way as when people are led to the Holy Spirit who will reveal within them, expose them, and show them what they really are. And by doing so, the Holy Spirit is able to do the transforming work according to the image of Christ. Hence, do not deprive them of this process of learning and the transforming work of God. Every problem a person has is always an opportunity for the Holy Spirit to transform that individual, but if we step in and substitute ourselves for the Holy Spirit by giving that person the solution, then we actually do a disservice to the Lord and to this person. Unfortunately, it is the greatest temptation for us all to lead the flock of God, for we realize one of the main functions of a shepherd or a pastor is to lead the flock. In this case, we just lead them to the Lord and nothing else. That is true shepherding of the flock. We are not to solve their problems by ourselves; that is not our work. But we are to lead them to the One and the only One who can truly solve their problems and lead them beside the still waters.

Sadly, this is so prevalent today that among God's people there are those who do not truly know the Person of the Holy Spirit. Even though some people may have received the baptism of the Holy Spirit, this term "baptism of the Holy Spirit" is a term that is wrongly used among God's people. I am not against it but it is a problem when people who have experienced the *power* of the Holy Spirit do not know the *Person* of the Holy Spirit. The Person of the Holy Spirit is so important. We don't just experience Him once or twice. He is the still waters, and we need to drink of Him daily, be refreshed by the Holy Spirit, and be transformed. In shepherding care the second thing we have to do is make them lie down in green pastures and lead them beside the still waters.

How many of us are doing that through the Holy Spirit? How anxious we all are to advise people! If people do not ask us for advice, we are still tempted to do so; but if they ask, of course, that is our great opportunity to go ahead and do so; nevertheless, we forget the Holy Spirit.

If from the very beginning of our involvement in pastoral care in caring for our brothers and sisters, we would lead them to the Holy Spirit instead of telling them what to do, then we will be with them through this process by praying together. Oftentimes we may know the answer, but we need to hold back from giving a person the answer right away. Rather, we should pray together with him, and after doing so, just wait and see if the Holy Spirit speaks to this person. Afterwards, we will fellowship with him and find out how he feels about this matter. Then we can either confirm it, if the person truly received the words from the Holy Spirit, or correct it, if this person is off-course. Since he does not have the experience of hearing the voice of the Spirit, he may misunderstand what He is saying. Well, that is what we need to do, but certainly we are not to take the place of the Holy Spirit. On the contrary, we have to lead them to the still waters, and that is true pastoral care.

Know the Restoration of the Lord

The third point: "He restoreth my soul." We realize that sheep are very temperamental. We as sheep oftentimes have our ups and downs. Sometimes we fall away or wander away and other times we might be wounded. Occasionally we are sick and we need to be restored. This word *restore* also can be translated "revive." We need to be revived. Sometimes our spirit is down and we feel miserable. We need to be revived. Other times we have fallen away and need to be restored which is a common thing with the sheep. Because this is common to the sheep, the one thing we have to do is restore and revive the sheep we are caring for. But if we ourselves are down, how can we revive our brothers and sisters? If we ourselves have fallen away we will be like the blind leading the blind and both will fall into the ditch. So that shows how important it is that we know the reviving of the Lord personally. We are not better than anyone else; we have our ups and downs as well. We have experienced falling away, we have gone through weaknesses, and we have gone through depressions. We have gone through all these things, but we find that our Lord has always revived and restored us. On the one hand, inasmuch as we have experienced all of what He has done for us, we can sympathize with those who need reviving or restoring. On the other hand, we can minister Christ, whom we have experienced ourselves as our restorer and our reviver in order to help our brothers and sisters to be restored and revived. Our Lord prayed for Peter that after he had been restored he would then be able to help others. We cannot restore others if we have never been restored before. The problem in pastoral care today is that some people are too strong. They may never have experienced being down or falling away or they may think that they have never had an evil thought. For this reason these people cannot sympathize with those who are emotionally down, who are feeling low, or who have been taken out. So sometimes we even hear people say, "Well, if they fall, let it be so." Then we just go on and leave them in a pitiful condition. When we hear someone saying this, we know that they are most likely those who are not real shepherds. If we are true shepherds of the Lord, we will never say such things.

In the book of Genesis chapter 33 Esau said to Jacob, "Let us take our journey and go on, and I will go before thee." And Jacob said to him, "My lord knows that the children are tender and the suckling sheep and kine are with me; and if they should overdrive them only one day all the flock would die. Let my Lord, I pray thee, pass on before his servant, and I will drive on at my ease according to the pace of the cattle that is before me and according to the pace of the children, until I come to my lord, to Seir" (vv. 12-14).

Even though Jacob was in a defensive mode when responding to Esau, he had the true spirit of a good shepherd when he said, "We cannot overdrive them." So when Esau said, "Let us take our journey together," and Jacob said, "No, no, no. You go before us, because you are on horseback, but I have all these young cattle and suckling children to tend for. And for this reason we have to go by their pace, for if we should overdrive them only one day, they will all die." Now that is a true shepherd's heart. But if we do not have the kind of shepherd-heart as Jacob, then we will never be able to really appreciate true shepherding. That is why we need to experience the ups and downs and the outcome of the Lord's dealings, as Jacob had, to know the restoration of the Lord.

Oftentimes, we may choose to go through some experiences on our own which is in the indirect will of God, but other times the experiences we had were chosen by God to have His way in us, because He wants to use us in His eternal work. If God does not want to use us in pastoral care, we do not need to go through these particular experiences; it will be much easier for us to go through our own way. But if we really want God to use us, we need to be prepared for His direct will to be done in us. We will go through much more difficulties than other believers. Perhaps we will chose not to go through these experiences, but it is indeed needed to equip us for this ministry of shepherding. It is surely needed; otherwise we do not have sympathy towards other people.

Again, a shepherd's heart is full of sympathy. Thus, without sympathy we are unable to enter into this pastoral care because that is the basic quality and requirement. We realize that to be a priest, to intercede for others, we need sympathy. Our Lord Jesus being our High Priest is full of sympathy, and this sympathy comes out of His own earthly experience. Even though He is the Son of God, He still had to learn obedience through the things which He suffered; therefore He is able to be the One who is able to save us to the uttermost. By all means I am not saying we have to fall into error before we can really help people who have fallen. In the case of our Lord Jesus, He never failed; even though He himself went through temptations and sufferings, He held fast to the end.

Now we come to another aspect within the area of restoration. We cannot always just deal with those healthy sheep; we have to deal with those disobedient, stubborn, fallen, wandering away, unhealthy sheep as well. Because they are the Lord's sheep, and the Lord loves them; so we have to take care of them. Just as the Lord said, "A shepherd will leave the ninety and nine sheep and go out and find the one wandering sheep" (see Luke 15:4). Sometimes we think He loves the wandering sheep more than the ninety-nine, and it does sometimes seem like that. Very often we find in a family, the parents seem to love a child that is always sick more than the other children who are healthy and strong. It is not that they are partial but it is because that child is sickly and needs more care; it comes naturally. And that is the way with the Lord. So one of the main functions of pastoral care is to restore the flock and bring them back to the Lord. Restoration means to bring His people back to the Lord. If God's people are not restored back to the Lord, it is not a true restoration. We may restore a person out of his predicament, but if he is not restored back to the Lord, he is not really restored in God's eye.

Walk in the Paths of Righteousness

The fourth point is, "He leadeth me in paths of righteousness for his name's sake." Occasionally we have to do the difficult work of restoring our fellow believers. We may think it is a waste of time taking care of all these troubled ones; instead we would rather take care of the healthy sheep and make them fat and happy. Why should we spend time with these sickly and poor wandering ones? Sometimes we may think it is a waste of time but with a shepherd's heart we will have a different attitude. We have to do lots of unpleasant work which may be negative. But after we have done it and restored our brothers and sisters then we will be able to continue to lead them. We have to lead them in the paths of righteousness for His name's sake. As we have mentioned before, in the ancient Middle-East countries a shepherd always walked before the sheep. He does not forcefully push the sheep; he gently leads them. We realize some shepherds overdrive the sheep, but in pastoral care we cannot hurry them. When we forcefully push them it is just like Jacob said, "If we overdrive them, they will die." If we lead them gently they will follow. In leading them, of course, we are ahead of them. In other words, we ourselves have to have the experience of walking in the paths of righteousness. Because we have walked in the paths of righteousness, so we can lead them.

Righteousness is something that we received freely when we first believed in the Lord, therefore Christ is our righteousness and we are clothed with Christ. And because He is our righteousness, we are able to stand before God because He sees His own Son, who is our righteousness. Thank God for that. But we will find the Scripture indicates that righteousness is more than just a door to salvation; righteousness is a path. And the path here in the original manuscript is plural—paths of righteousness; in other words, they cover the practical side of our walk as well. It does not only refer to our initial justification in Christ, but here the righteousness we are talking about refers to the righteousnesses of the saints (see Revelation 19:8). Those saints who are the bride of Christ are clothed with bright, white, shining linen which is the righteousnesses of the saints. Also we find in the first book of John chapter 2:29, "If ye know that he is righteous, know that everyone who practices righteousness is begotten of him." After we are made righteous then we have to walk in the paths of righteousness for His name's sake. Otherwise, if we do not walk in the paths of righteousness, then the name of the Lord will be disgraced. We are supposed to be righteous, for we have been made righteous in Christ, and if we do not walk in the paths of righteousness, people will say, "Now what is this all about?" Therefore, we must walk in the paths of righteousness. This is not only for our own sake. If it is only for our sake, it may well become self-righteousness and we may boast of ourselves. Instead it should be for His great name's sake. To put it in a very simple way, it means that we give God all His rights. That is righteousness. We believe totally in Him because He is our God and our Lord. Also, He is our Majesty and King. He has every right over our lives. So are we walking in the paths of righteousness? Do we give Him His rightful place every day of our lives? Let us put it another way. Are we doing the will of God? When our Lord Jesus was on earth, He used His physical body to do the will of God. We belong to the Lord and have presented our bodies as a living sacrifice. In this case, are we using our body to do the will of God? Do we give Him His rights and let His will prevail in our daily life? If we do, then we are walking in the paths of righteousness for His name's sake. As a result, the name of the Lord will be honored and people will see and glorify the heavenly Father. This is another area of pastoral care. We have to lead our brothers and sisters in the paths of righteousness.

This is an unrighteous world that we are living in and people are getting more and more unrighteous. Therefore, we have to walk in the paths of righteousness so that we may be a testimony of God to the world; otherwise we fail in our testimony. Many of God's people are living according to the standard of this world; we cannot even distinguish the difference between the two. We know we are saved, God knows we are saved, but the world does not know. They say we are no different from them because we do the same thing as they do. It is so very important to help God's beloved ones and lead them in the paths of righteousness for His name's sake. But again we cannot lead if we ourselves are not walking in it. It is important that we go before them as we have already mentioned, because a shepherd is to be an example to the sheep. We walk before them and they will follow.

"Thou Art with Me"

The fifth point is: "Yea, though I walk through the valley of the shadow of death, I will fear no evil: for thou art with me" (Psalm 23:4). Brothers and sisters, we all will go through periods of a low state in our lives—depressed, hurt, wandering away—and spiritually we all will go through the valley of the shadow of death. Some books indicate that in the region of Palestine there is a place called "the valley of the shadow of death." It is said that when shepherds lead the sheep from one pasture to another, they often go through such a deep valley that the sun cannot shine through to its depth, so it is called "the valley of the shadow of death." I do not know how true that is, but we will find from our experience that God has not promised we will never have this "valley experience." We realize that God's people do sometimes go through "valley experiences," but remember that it is "the valley of the shadow of death." In other words, it is not death; it is just a shadow. It may frighten us but it cannot hurt us spiritually. We realize God's people do go through these experiences. For example, maybe a tragic thing has happened in the family or there is a death of someone close to us or maybe a traumatic experience happened to someone we love, and it is as if the sheep are going through "the valley of the shadow of death." When these situations occur, how does the function of pastoral care take place? David said, "Though I walk through the valley of the shadow of death, I shall fear no evil." Why? Because "Thou art with me." In other words, pastoral care means we are there in time of need for our brothers and sisters. We will make ourselves available. In as much as people go through these times of tragic experiences, we may not have any words to comfort them. In fact, our words cannot comfort them and may even become a disservice to them. Instead, our very presence in being with them and available to them will strengthen, comfort, and help them through this period of the shadow of death. The key for the work of pastoral care is to make ourselves available. Any time there is a need, we should be there. We will never say, "Well, it is already eleven o'clock in the evening; please call me tomorrow morning." We need to recognize that being with those in times of need is true pastoral care. Do not think that in doing pastoral care we must say something to comfort or strengthen these hurting people. Oftentimes, not saying anything is better than saying something. If we say some unfit words, we will be like the three friends of Job who made the situation worse. All we need to do is be there for them because our very presence will comfort them.

Strengthening the Sheep

The sixth point is: "I will fear no evil: for thou art with me; thy rod and thy staff, they comfort me" (Psalm 23:4b). We know the rod in the Scripture means several things. The rod can be a protection against the lion, the bear or the wolves. In the spiritual sense we need to protect our fellow believers from the assault of the enemy—deception, heresy, lies, false teaching, etc. And also the rod can be used for counting the sheep just to be sure each one under his care is there and not lost because every single one of them is dear to the shepherd. Spiritually speaking we need to be always mindful of them to make sure that none is wandering away from the Lord, because every one of them is dear to the Lord. Sometimes the rod can be used for discipline when the sheep wander away and need to be brought back to the flock. In the spiritual sense, sometimes they have fallen into sin or made mistakes; therefore, with the leading of the Holy Spirit we will gently correct or admonish them and restore them. We know that the staff is used to rescue the sheep which may have fallen into the ditch. Under these circumstances the shepherd will use a staff, which has a hook that can pull them out from where they have fallen. Spiritually speaking, we sometimes need to use a staff to help our fellow believers, who may have fallen away from the Lord, so that we can restore their spiritual condition.

"Thy rod and Thy staff, they comfort me" (v. 4b). Comfort means more than just a comforting feeling; it really means strengthening. One of the main functions of the work of the shepherd is to strengthen his sheep; therefore we as shepherds need to do the same.

Claim the Victory of Christ

The seventh point is: "Thou preparest a table before me in the presence of mine enemies" (Psalm 23:5a). Now I would like to apply this particular verse in a different way from the common interpretation and share with you the way I understand it. We realize that a shepherd is to prepare a table because obviously the sheep cannot prepare the table for themselves. And the shepherd has to prepare the table in the presence of their enemies. Maybe it indicates a physical wolf which may be hiding in the woods, but because the shepherd is there guarding and protecting the sheep they are able to feed upon the pasture without any fear of the wolf, because a table has been prepared for them before their enemies. They have nothing to fear because the shepherd is there for them.

But I would like to apply this in a different way. Our Lord Jesus defeated the enemy on the cross and made him His spoil, which has become our food. We recall the story of Caleb and Joshua. The Israelites were ready at Kadesh Barnea to enter into the land flowing with milk and honey. His servant Moses sent twelve spies to spy out the land. Ten of them came back and said: "We cannot go in because there are giants dwelling in the land with walled cities. They will swallow us up" (See Numbers 13:28). But Caleb and Joshua said, "No, the Lord is going to give them to us and they shall be our food" (See Numbers 14:8-9). In other words, we will eat them up which will make us stronger spiritually. The victory of Christ on Calvary's cross is complete, so that we can sit at the table which He has spread before our enemies and be satisfied. It is so very true that His victory is our victory and the enemies become our food. In our life's journey with God as His sheep we sometimes go through periods of ups and downs, or through periods of reviving, or through periods of the shadow of death. Even though we experience all these sometimes we forget that we have enemies. God's enemies are our enemies and they are around us all the time. Satan is trying to swallow us and eat us up whenever he has opportunities to do so.

Dear brothers and sisters, we need to enter into spiritual reality in order to experience the victory of Christ ourselves. As we experience the victory of Christ—though we may still go through crises because the enemy is always trying to swallow us up—once we claim the victory of Christ, the enemy becomes our food. We are strengthened after we have experienced that spiritual conflict. It is because of the victory of Christ that we are strengthened spiritually. This is the meaning of the table spread before the enemy. We who have tasted the victory of Christ over our enemy are able to prepare such a table for our brothers and sisters in the presence of the enemy in the time of their needs. We can really help them, comfort them, and show them that they do not need to be afraid. They can enter into the victory of Christ as well, because the enemy is a defeated foe. And as they go through this growing process we will find they have been strengthened as if they had been at the table spread for them. This is something we need to prepare for them before their enemies. But before we can help anyone in this aspect, we have to have had first-hand experience ourselves, and then we are able to help others.

Filled with the Holy Spirit

The eighth point is: "Thou hast anointed my head with oil; my cup runneth over" (Psalm 23:5b). I remember once I was told that in the Orient before the night falls the shepherd will begin to gather the sheep with his rod and count them. He will then examine the sheep one by one in case some of them have been wounded which normally occurs on their head. The reason for their injury is that while they are grazing in the pasture sometimes they accidentally get into thorn bushes or thistle bushes and are torn by them. So the shepherd will have ointment ready to apply to the wound to heal them. Sometimes when sheep have a fever the shepherd will dip their heads into a bucket of cold water and the water overflows just as the cup runs over. This is to help them to lower the fever. Now we are told that probably these are the things done in the olden days, but I will apply it in a different way. Spiritually speaking, of course, we know oil always speaks of the Holy Spirit. "And anoint my head with oil" (see v.5b), simply means to be filled with the Holy Spirit.

Today we need to help our brothers and sisters. This is part of pastoral care. When we take care of the sheep, we are not only to see that they have food to eat and water to drink, we also have to make sure that they are restored from all their weariness, and able to walk in the paths of righteousness. They are able to go through the "valley experience" and not be ashamed or defeated or frightened, for they can rest in the presence of their enemies. But that is only part of the responsibility of those who shepherd them. They are to also help them to enter into the fullness of the Spirit. Being filled with the Holy Spirit means to be constantly ruled by the Holy Spirit. Therefore, those who are under our care need to know and live a life under the rule of the Holy Spirit. We have to bring them to that experience. Now if we do not bring them to that condition, we have not taken care of them completely. It will not be complete unless we lead them into a life that is ruled by the Holy Spirit. Then those dear ones of the Lord will be established. To be filled with the Holy Spirit is not just a one-time event; it is not even an experience of a few times. To be filled with the Holy Spirit should be a constant filling. If we are constantly being ruled by the Holy Spirit, then we ourselves are then able to help our brothers and sisters to experience the filling of the Holy Spirit. All the above that we have mentioned are included in pastoral care. All these things are what the Lord as our Shepherd is doing for us and doing through us to His people.

Consequences of Shepherding

If we are engaged in this pastoral care, these are the things that we should do. And when these things are as they ought to be what will be the consequences? Firstly, "My cup runneth over." The sheep's cup runs over because the sheep are so satisfied with the abundant care; hence, they are abundantly satisfied and their cup is running over.

Secondly, "Surely, goodness and loving-kindness shall follow me all the days of my life" (Psalm 23:6a). In other words, the sheep enter into a sense of assurance knowing that the Lord will take care of them throughout their lives; for every single experience they had of the Lord strengthened their assurance in the Lord. The Lord has been so faithful and gracious to all of us. Therefore we know that the sheep will say, "Now I know the Lord is so faithful that 'surely goodness and mercy shall follow me all the days of my life,"' because He has brought me thus far. He has proven His loving-kindness and tender mercy to me, so I know He will follow me all the days of my life.

When a Christian comes to this point; he is satisfied within himself and he has such trust and confidence in the Lord.

Thirdly, "And I will dwell in the house of Jehovah for the length of the days" (Psalm 23:6b). We will find that the sheep are happy to be in the house of the Lord. We realize that there are many people who are not satisfied or happy to "dwell in the house of the Lord"; they have never really felt at home. But those who really have been taken care of in this fashion will feel at home and at rest in the house of God. They will be happy and get along with brothers and sisters whom they gather with. They are satisfied and have confidence in the Lord. Now these are the results of pastoral care as the Lord desires us to have.

As we have gone through this Psalm, we have found that the Lord is our Shepherd, and He has shepherded us in this way and is calling all of us into this pastoral care in the body of Christ. It is not that we can do it ourselves, for He has done it for us and is able to do it through us to other people.

In the New Testament we often say that the books of First and Second Timothy and the book of Titus are pastoral letters; that is commonly accepted among God's people. These three books are pastoral letters because Paul was writing to two young brothers who were serving in the area of pastoral care and was advising them.

Actually I feel that all the letters in the New Testament are pastoral letters. We can go through them one by one and feel that every letter has something to do with pastoral care. For instance, the book of Romans no doubt is: "He made me lie down in green pastures." For there he shows us the riches of the glory of our salvation in Jesus Christ. How we are delivered from sin and death and filled with His life and glory. And the book of I Corinthians will surprise us: "He leads me beside still waters." The sheep there were in such turbulence and Paul was trying to direct them to the still waters. But if we go through every single letter in the New Testament we will find each letter gives us a different phase or a certain aspect of pastoral care. The Lord being our Shepherd is so good, caring and loving to us. He expects us to take up this function of pastoral care in the body of Christ. Then the body will really be healthy and satisfied and have confidence in the Lord.

Dear heavenly Father, we want to declare with David that You are truly our Shepherd and we shall not want. We do praise and thank You for what You have done for us in the past. You have proven Yourself to us as the Good Shepherd, the Great Shepherd and the Chief Shepherd. Now, oh Lord, You have called us to join with You in this care of Your flock. We acknowledge that we are totally inadequate, but our adequacy is in You. We thank You for what You have already done in us, so we just offer ourselves to You that You may be able to do the same thing in our dear brothers and sisters through us. Lord, we will consider it such a great honor and privilege if You will use us in this way, but just keep us humble before You, knowing that without You we can do nothing, but with You all things are possible. We ask in the name of our Lord Jesus. Amen.

Chapter 3

The Character of the Shepherd

Dear Lord, we do praise and thank You for gathering us in Your presence these few days. Lord, we thank You You truly are our Good Shepherd. You have been taking care of us in such a way that we do not even know what to say. We truly desire to worship You and tell You that we do appreciate everything You have done for us. Our only desire is that You will draw from us that which is Your due, Your right. Oh, by Your love constrain us so that we have to offer ourselves as a living sacrifice. We want You to take hold of us and do with us according to Your heart's desire. Lord, we want You to be glorified. We want You to be exalted and for people to be able to see and hear You through us. So we commit this time again into Your hands and trust Your Holy Spirit to open Your word to us and open our hearts to Your word, that these may not be just words but by the power of Your Spirit they may be life and spirit to us. We ask in the name of our Lord Jesus. Amen.

John 21:15-19: "When therefore they had dined, Jesus says to Simon Peter, Simon, [son] of Jonas, lovest thou me more than these? He says to him, Yea, Lord; thou knowest that I am attached to thee. He says to him, Feed my lambs. He says to him again a second time, Simon, [son] of Jonas, lovest thou me? He says to him, Yea, Lord; thou knowest that I am attached to thee. He says to him,

Shepherd my sheep. He says to him the third time, Simon, [son] of Jonas, art thou attached to me? Peter was grieved because he said to him the third time, Art thou attached to me? And said to him, Lord, thou knowest all things; thou knowest that I am attached to thee. Jesus says to him, Feed my sheep. Verily, verily, I say to thee, When thou wast young, thou girdest thyself, and walkedst where thou desiredst; but when thou shalt be old, thou shalt stretch forth thy hands, and another shall gird thee, and bring thee where thou dost not desire. But he said this signifying by what death he should glorify God. And having said this, he says to him, Follow me."

I Peter 5:1-4: "The elders which (are] among you I exhort, who [am their] fellow-elder and witness of the sufferings of the Christ, who also [am] partaker of the glory about to be revealed: shepherd the flock of God which [is] among you, exercising oversight, not by necessity, but willingly; not for base gain, but readily; not as lording it over your possessions, but being models for the flock. And when the chief shepherd is manifested ye shall receive the unfading crown of glory."

In the past two sessions we have shared together on this matter of pastoral care in the body of Christ. We find that pastoral care is one of the greatest needs among God's people today. God has given to the church some pastors and teachers and whenever we see this gift functioning we thank God for it. Also, we find that God has entrusted to the elders of the local assembly the shepherding of His dear ones who are in these local assemblies. We thank God for their labor. But we see that this matter of shepherding is so essential to the body of Christ that God not only has given us these two classes of people to do this work, but the shepherding work actually is to be carried out by all the members of the body of Christ. We as members of one another are to take care of each other. In the house of God no one member in the body can say, "I am just going to take care of myself; I do not have to worry or care about the other members." It cannot be done this way, because God puts us together in the body as members one of another. We cannot say, "I have no need of ears or other parts of the body." We have to take care of one another; so in a sense, so far as this function is concerned, it is actually to be done by all the members of the body of Christ. If this function is really manifested in the church, then it will be built in love. Consequently, there will be growth and blessing and it will give glory to God among His people.

We also shared together on the work of a shepherd which is the work of pastoral care. What are the works involved? We find in Psalm 23 all these different aspects of works—to make the sheep lie down in green pastures, to lead them beside the still waters, to restore their souls, to lead them in the paths of righteousness for His name's sake. He goes with them through the valley of the shadow of death and sometimes has to use the rod and staff. He spreads a table in the presence of their enemies and anoints their heads with oil. In other words, all these are various aspects of the *work* of pastoral care. Now we would like to look into this matter of the *character* of the shepherd.

Peter Called to be a Shepherd

We are familiar with the story mentioned in the Gospel according to John, chapter 21. We recall that Peter is a fisherman. He was a fisherman by trade; he cast nets to catch fish. Then one day as the Lord was walking by the Sea of Galilee, Peter was casting nets, and the Lord said, "Come and follow Me and I will make you fishers of men" (see Matthew 4:19). We know Peter as a fisherman had to be brave, courageous, decisive, rough, strong and skillful. These are the expected characteristics of a fisherman and it really fits the temperament of Peter. By temperament he is that kind of person—impulsive, outspoken, simple but brave, bold. We find the Lord called him to be a fisher of men, not a fisher of fish. On the day of Pentecost we find Peter casting the net and catching three thousand souls. Again, we will find in the house of Cornelius, he cast the net and his whole household was caught; that was Peter the fisherman. That was his calling. In a sense, we can say he was an evangelist which was a gift from God. We recall Peter was also an apostle, but the Bible does not indicate what the specific gift of an apostle should be. We only know that an apostle is an office; it is a commission, but what the gift of an apostle is we do not know. So maybe the gift of an apostle is an evangelizing gift. Here we find that Peter had this gift of evangelizing or of casting nets to catch souls for the Lord. But rarely do we think of Peter as a shepherd, but actually he was not only called to be a fisher of men; he was also called by the Lord to be a shepherd. At the beginning, the Lord called him to be a fisher of men while our Lord was still on earth. After the resurrection of our Lord Jesus, Peter was called again by the Lord to be a shepherd of his people.

The calling came in this fashion. One day Peter had nothing to do. All that we know is that he was an active person; he could not stay home and do nothing, he had to do something. After the Lord's resurrection and before His ascension, the Lord suddenly appeared and disappeared many times before His disciples, and they never knew when the Lord would appear again. Therefore Peter could not wait anymore; he had to do something, so he said, "I go fishing." And six other disciples said, "Well, why don't we go together with you" (see John 21:1-3). So they all went fishing; but they fished the whole night and caught nothing from their labor. Peter was a master fisherman, but he could not catch any fish that night. Then in the early dawn the Lord was standing on the shore and said, "Do you have anything to eat?" They said, "We have not caught anything." So the Lord said, "Cast the net on the right side of the ship and you will find." They did as the Lord directed them and they caught a net full of fish. After this discourse with the Lord, they did not know that it was Jesus. They could not recognize the Lord because they were still some distance away from the shore; and in the early dawn probably there was a mist or fog. But immediately, John perceived it was the Lord, so John said, "It is the Lord." And we can see how impulsive Peter was. He right away put a coat upon himself and jumped into the water and swam to the shore; that was the Peter we are familiar with. After all seven of the disciples came up to the shore, they saw the Lord had already prepared breakfast for them; there was not only bread but fish as well. We are certain that one day we will all dine with the Lord at His second coming. But that morning the Lord let them enjoy breakfast with Him as a foretaste of what is to come. After they finished breakfast then the Lord began to speak to Peter (see John 21:4-9).

We remember when Peter denied the Lord three times in the night that the Lord was being arrested, he went out completely devastated over what he had done to the Lord whom he loved. But after the resurrection of the Lord, we recall that He appeared to Peter alone. And I do believe by appearing to Peter alone, the Lord restored Peter, but not publicly (see Mark 16:7). So in a sense this incident did not refer to the full restoration of Peter's faith. Sometimes we explain this incident and say, "Well, the Lord has already restored Peter"; but the fact of the matter is the Lord wanted to restore him before his companions. In other words, so far as his relationship with the Lord, Peter was restored, but in his companion's view, they still had some questions about him. So that was the reason why the Lord used this opportunity to restore him before his companions; for he denied the Lord three times so the Lord asked him three times, "Do you love me?" And that seems to balance it out and clear the whole situation (see John 21:15).

Sometimes we wonder if the Lord's action is necessary; but to me I feel this incident is very important and necessary. Why? Because the application actually is that the Lord was going to commission Peter to a further work. Originally, He had called Peter to be a fisher of men, but now the risen Lord was going to call Peter to a further work—not one of just casting the nets and bringing people to himself but also to shepherd His flock. And this incident that happened to Peter was the preparation for the Lord's calling him to be a shepherd for the Lord's flock.

Love: the Essential Quality of Shepherding

As we read this account in the Scripture, we find that the Lord emphasized one point again and again, and that is love. The most essential character of a shepherd is love. Without love we cannot do the work of shepherding. There can be no pastoral care if there is no love in the heart of the person who does the care; therefore, love is the foundation of this pastoral care function. Love is the most important quality and essential character in the life of a shepherd or whoever is doing pastoral care.

"Feed My Lambs"

In the Gospel according to John chapter 21:15-17 the Lord says, "Simon, son of Jonas, do you love me more than these?" Now what are "these"? Do we remember the fire at the seashore of Tiberias where Jesus appeared again to

His disciples who had been fishing all night without catching anything? We also recall that when Peter denied the Lord he was by the fire because it was a cold night. He followed the Lord at a distance and drew near to the fire to warm himself. We know too that Peter loved a crowd of people; he did not like to be alone. So even when our Lord was being judged, there was Peter close to the fire and in the midst of the crowd.

Let us go back to the incident at the seashore of Tiberias, where the Lord asked him: "Peter, do you love Me more than these?" What the Lord was saying is this: "Do you love Me more than the fire? Do you love Me more than your companions? Do you love Me more than the bread and the fish? So do you love Me more than all these?" We know that all these things represent something that appeals to us naturally. In other words, these things gratify our self or our flesh if we have them excessively. We need warmth and comfort. We also enjoy companions. We cannot live without food. We need all of the above. These things will gratify our physical bodies, but anyone who loves these things more than the Lord, evidently loves himself. It is as if the Lord is saying, "Do you love me more than yourself?"

Once upon a time Peter thought that he loved the Lord more than himself, but it was proven that this was not the case (see Luke 22:31-34). Surely he loved himself more than the Lord, so the Lord said, "Do you really love Me more than these?" In other words, "Do you really love Me more than loving yourself? Are you self-centered or are you Christ-centered?" The love of God cannot be compared to anything or any other kind of love. So the Lord began with these questions: "Peter, do you love Me more than these?" Even though the word love is *agape* in Greek, it is that absolute love. But we find that it is being compared with something else. Peter said, "Lord, You know I love You." And in the Darby translation it says, "I am attached to You," because the word Peter used is not *agape*; it is *phileo* in Greek. In other words, I am friendly with You; I am really for You; I have a good feeling about You. Perhaps Peter remembered his own failure when he said: "If other people desert You, I will follow You even unto death; I love You more than anything else." But in reality he denied the Lord three times. After this incident, he dare not say any more because he knew he did not have that absolute love towards the Lord and he also knew he loved himself more than his Lord. He had learned his lesson through his failure. He said, "Lord, I am attached to You; I really do feel affection for You; I am friendly with You." Then the Lord said, "Feed my lambs." We will find the commission of our Lord Jesus to Peter is upon this matter of love. In other words, if there is not absolute love that loves the Lord more than these things or more than loving ourselves, we are unfit for any pastoral care. The Lord will not commit any lamb to us because we only care for ourselves and not for other people. In case any sheep or lamb should be committed to us we will be like hired workers but not shepherds. We will probably feed upon the lambs instead of feeding the lambs. So when the wolf comes, we will leave the lambs behind and just take care of ourselves.

Dear brothers and sisters, as long as we are self-centered, as long as we love ourselves more than anything else, as long as we love comfort and ease, as long as we love to gratify our flesh, more than the Lord, the Lord will never commit any lamb to us. We may try to feed them in our own way, but the result is we will hurt them instead of helping them. Love is the prerequisite of shepherding; but our love towards one another is so limited, therefore the Lord said to Peter, "Feed my lambs."

Now lambs are little sheep that need to be fed because they are not able to digest solid food. They can only take in pre-digested food, such as milk. In other words, we have to digest the food through patience and love and out of what is digested in us, we are able to feed the lambs. Normally those who have been saved for some time ought to be able to take solid food and feed the lambs. We remember in the Scriptures that if a person has believed in the Lord for a few years he ought to be able to take solid food (see 1 Corinthians 2-3; Hebrews 5-6). He ought to have his "senses exercised, distinguishing good and evil" (Hebrews 5:14). His spiritual senses should be exercised, and he should be able to digest solid food himself and be able to feed the little lambs.

Now we can see that love is the first requirement; even though our love towards other people seems limited, if we love our Lord more than ourselves, then we are able to love God's children.

"Shepherd the Sheep"

Then the Lord asked Peter the second time: "Simon, son of Jonas, do you love Me?" And here we find that the Lord put it in such a way that there was no comparison to what the Lord had said before to Peter: "Do you love Me more than these?" For the Lord is not comparing himself with anything else this time. Why? Because the Lord is incomparable. We cannot put Him on the same level with anybody or with anything else because He is unique.

In the Gospel according to Matthew chapter 17 we recall that on the Mount of Transfiguration when Moses and Elijah appeared with Jesus that Peter put them on the same footing as our Lord. Surely, Moses was the greatest law-giver while Elijah was the representative of all the prophets, and Peter tried to put them as equal to the Lord. Immediately, God cut him off and said: "No; this is my beloved Son in whom I am well pleased; hear Him." Then Moses and Elijah disappeared before the disciples because the Lord Jesus is incomparable. We cannot compare Him with anyone—not even among the greatest. "They saw no one but Jesus alone" (see Matthew 17:8). So the Lord said, "Now do you love Me?" There was no longer any comparison to Him with anything else. The Lord should be everything; He is all and in all. And because Peter had already learned of himself, he dared not again to say he loved the Lord in such an absolute way. He could only say, "Lord, You know I am attached to You; I really feel good about You." And on that basis the Lord said, "Shepherd my sheep."

Among the flock of God there are baby sheep such as lambs, but we also have full-grown sheep. Therefore, we do not feed these sheep; we shepherd them. We know there is a great difference between feeding and shepherding. Feeding means we feed them with pre-digested food; we will have to first digest the food for them. For instance, when we study the word of God, it will be illuminated through the Holy Spirit so that we can digest it and it becomes living in us and enables us to absorb it. And out of our experiential understanding of the word of God in our daily living, we are able to feed the lambs. So our supply will help brothers and sisters who are not able to chew solid food. But at the same time we do not feed the full-grown sheep with the pre-digested food. The problem is that oftentimes we feed the sheep in general without distinguishing between sheep and lambs. If we treat them the same way by feeding milk to the grown-up sheep then they will go backwards spiritually. They will remain babes instead of growing up in the Lord which is the reason why today we find the word of God is so foreign to God's people; because they do not go to the word themselves. They do not listen to the Spirit themselves. They do not have intimate communion with the Lord themselves. They do not take their problems to the Lord and seek after Him. They do not look to the Holy Spirit to illumine the word to them personally; instead, we find that they are just waiting for someone to feed them every Sunday. They come to be fed with food that has already been digested. They do not need to meditate upon the word nor do they need to deal with it. They just listen and if the message suits them, they are happy; if it does not, they reject it. They cannot digest the solid food; it all has to be pre-digested. It is no wonder today that there are so many babes in the church. The responsibility is mutual between the shepherd and the sheep, because it lies not only with those who are supposed to be seeking the food as they should, but it also lies with those who shepherd them who are trying to do everything for the sheep. It seems like we never give them a chance to digest or solve problems for themselves. The most we do is to make them lie down in green pastures, let them feed upon the grass, let them chew the cud, let them rest and drink. But rather the most important thing is to direct them, to lead their way and when they fall away, restore them; and also to be with them when they go through difficulties. That is all we need to do instead of doing everything for them. We carry the lambs in our arms, but with the sheep we lead the way. We do not carry them; we shepherd them.

As we have already mentioned before, the most essential thing in shepherding the sheep demands absolute love towards the Lord. If we love the Lord absolutely then when the Lord says, "Shepherd my sheep," we will do it glad-heartedly. We realize that shepherding the sheep is more difficult than feeding the lambs, because the sheep have their own thinking, their own will and their own way. Therefore, they will not stay in our arms and allow us to help them because oftentimes they do not appreciate or agree with us. They argue, murmur, and criticize us. So it is more difficult to shepherd the sheep, but we need to bear and forbear with them and not be heavy-handed. We know that God respects our personality. Consequently, we have to respect their personality and try to help them, shepherd them, lead them, and it requires that absolute love towards the Lord.

"Feed My Sheep"

The Lord does not stop there, because among the flock of God there are not only lambs and sheep but also sick sheep. These sick sheep are grown-up sheep, and yet spiritually they are no longer pursuing the Lord. They have declined and are weakened. For this reason they are unable to take care of themselves. This is not only physically true, this is also spiritually true. Among God's people there are some who have been with the Lord for a good number of years, but somehow, spiritually, they begin to grow old, weak, and stagnant. They have stopped pursuing the Lord and have become passive. So the Lord said, "Peter, are you attached to Me?" Instead of demanding absolute love from Peter, the Lord pleaded with him. Consequently the Lord said, "Are you really attached to Me? Are you friendly to Me, feel good about Me?" And when the Lord said that, of course, Peter was very grieved because he knew that he could not rise up to that standard. He wanted to love the Lord, but he dare not boast anymore. He was grieved and said, "Lord, You know everything. You know I am attached to You." So on that basis the Lord said, "Feed my sheep." We know by now that some but not all sheep need feeding. Ordinarily, sheep only need shepherding, but when some sheep get old, sick or weak, then we need to feed them even though it is more difficult to do so. For these sheep had past experience with the Lord, also with their long past history they have been molded in a certain form and are not very flexible. At the time when we try to feed them, they do not appreciate it at all. They think they should feed us. So they will say, "Who are you?" Thus, it is more difficult to feed the aged, sick, and experienced ones than the baby Christians. Here we see Peter, a fisherman—strong, rough, and impulsive. He would never be able to feed the sheep, especially the sick, aged, and experienced Christians. He would be very frustrated with them and have no sympathy with them. If someone was weak and under Peter's care, he would not be able to care for them because he was strong-willed and rough. Thus, it took his fall to humble him and make him sympathetic towards others. So when Peter said, "Lord, I am attached to You," the Lord said, "now I am ready to commit the old and sick sheep under your care; you can feed them."

Not Natural Love, But Divine Love

Brothers and sisters, one of the most important characteristics that shepherds must have is love. Do not think that we have that love; for our natural love is not enough. It is not only inadequate, but it can really spoil the whole work of God. It has to be the love of God. At first Peter thought he had that love, but he discovered he did not. However, when he realized that he did not have it and was willing to acknowledge it, then he was given that love.

Every time we think we have God's love we truly do not know what that love is. Once we really feel that we do not have that love and we acknowledge it before the Lord, the Lord will then give us that love. This can only come from the Lord, which is the reason He asked Peter that question: "Do you love Me?" This love does not begin in us. We cannot generate or manufacture it; if it is so, it will not be God's love. When we focus our eyes upon the Lord, and Him alone, we will be constrained by the love of Christ, and it will be given to us and enable us to love.

Whenever we are doing this pastoral care, let us realize that this is not something that can be done out of our own strength. It is more than just a matter of solving problems; it is more than a matter of helping in certain ways, but behind pastoral care, there must be love. If love is not there, even though we help our brothers and sisters to solve their problems and even provide them with something to ease their difficulties, we cannot consider this as pastoral care because it does not result in the glory of God. Instead, we may get the glory. For this reason, it does not bring people to the Lord but ourselves. Because of this, we have to have the love which is from our Lord whenever we are shepherding our brothers and sisters. We have to ask the Lord to fill us with His love day by day. Once we are filled with His love, then we are able to feed the lambs, shepherd the sheep and feed the sick and aged sheep.

Share in the Non-Atoning Sufferings of Christ

> "The elders which [are] among you I exhort, who [am their] fellow-elder and witness of the sufferings of the Christ, who also [am] partaker of the glory about to be revealed" (I Peter 5:1).

This indicates that Peter was a fellow-elder among them. We understand that out of the twelve apostles, some of them also became elders in the church. Peter was one of them and John was another, because in the second and third books of John he said: "John the elder." We realize that there are different interpretations, but I personally feel that it can be both at the same time. John was an aged person at the time he wrote the first and second books of John, and he was probably an elder in the church in Jerusalem. During that time the church in Jerusalem was the center of the Lord's work. So it was more than just a local assembly. We can see that the apostles not only lived there but also ministered to the church there. And we also believe that there were some among them who served as elders of the church in Jerusalem at that time.

For instance, Peter was an elder in the church in Jerusalem and was also called to shepherd the flock there. But not only was he called to be a shepherd of the local flock in Jerusalem, he was also called to shepherd the whole flock of God. I believe that since Peter was an apostle and elder in the church, he travelled around among the assemblies and his shepherding actually covered a much wider area.

When he wrote to the elders who were shepherding the flock in the different assemblies, he said, "I am your fellow-elder and witness of the sufferings of the Christ" (see I Peter 5:1a). He shows us that being an elder in the church and the sufferings of Christ are inseparable. Many of those among God's people would like to be elders, but let me tell you, suffering cannot be separated from the eldership. If you do not want suffering, do not aspire to be an elder. You can live a more comfortable life if you are not an elder. If you desire to be an elder then be prepared to be a witness of the sufferings of the Christ. The word "witness" in the original meaning is "martyr". You must be ready to be persecuted and killed; ready to share in the sufferings of Christ.

We know the sufferings of Christ are so inclusive, but there is one part of His sufferings that we cannot share with Him; Christ died as our substitute. His was an atoning death and He tread the winepress alone. No one was with Him, and no one could be with Him. So far as that part of His suffering is concerned, He was alone. We may receive the benefit of His sufferings, but we cannot share His sufferings in this particular part. But there is another part of His sufferings which we are called to have fellowship with, and we need to be very clear about it. On the one hand, we cannot share in His sufferings which is His atoning death. He died for us and we have received the benefit of it. We thank God for that! But on the other hand, there is a wide area of the sufferings of Christ that we are to fellowship and share with Him. This witness of the sufferings of Christ does not mean that we are just standing there witnessing, as if we are watching what is happening to Him. Of course, that is true, we have to see that first; but once we see that, we are called into this fellowship with His sufferings. In other words, we are not just standing there observing it, we are drawn into it and we become a part of it as a martyr. We have to suffer for it which is to die to ourselves. Therefore, shepherding and suffering cannot be separated. The only reason that we can endure suffering is because there is love in it. Love and suffering are inseparable. Whenever there is love, there is bound to be suffering. For instance, parents love their children and they have to suffer for them. Love always includes suffering. If we do not love, we do not need to suffer. God so loved the world that He suffered in giving up His only begotten Son. No one can realize how much God suffered from it; just as Christ loves the church and gave himself for her. For He laid down His life for the sheep, and how much He suffered for that love.

Sometimes we think of the sufferings of Christ only in the area of the physical side, but that is the least part of it. His greatest suffering was on the cross. We remember He said: “My God, My God why hast Thou forsaken me?” (Matthew 27:46b) He was equal with God, co-existent from eternity, always One, and never separated from each other. But when Jesus was on the cross during those last three hours, the Father and Son were separated. Jesus suffered a great deal from the separation; but why did the Father allow this to happen? "Why hast Thou forsaken me?" The only answer is love, because God loves us and gave His only begotten Son, and that is why.

Therefore, whoever is to do the work of shepherding must have the will and the mindset to suffer. If we are not ready to suffer, we should not be involved in the work of shepherding; we will not be able to stand or endure it. But if there is the love of God, then love suffers long. We remember the apostle Paul said in the book of Colossians chapter 1:24, "Now, I rejoice in sufferings for you." Why is it so? Because he said, "I fill up that which is behind of the tribulations of Christ in my flesh for His body which is the assembly."

Through the sufferings of Christ or the atoning death of Christ, the church was born, but for the church to be built up and to arrive full-grown, in the measure of the stature of the fullness of the Christ, we will find that God uses His redeemed ones to fill up that which is behind of the afflictions of Christ for His body's sake. To Paul, being an apostle, of course, this was part of his work to fill up that which is behind of the afflictions of Christ for His body's sake. And through such fellowship with His sufferings, there will be something brought forth out of it that will last for eternity, and be part of that mature body of Christ.

The apostle Peter, who was a shepherd himself, also knew what it was to suffer, and he exhorted us by saying, "Be ready to suffer."

Exercising Oversight

> "Shepherd the flock of God which [is] among you, exercising oversight, not by necessity, but willingly; not for base gain, but readily; not as lording it over your possessions, but being models for the flock" (I Peter 5:2-3).

On that basis of having a mind to suffer Peter exhorted the elders of the church to exercise oversight over the flock of God. Now by exercising oversight, it does not mean we do everything for them. It means that we oversee them. But with the lambs, of course, we have to feed them but with the sheep we just direct them unless they are the sickly or aged sheep.

The problem today is caused by the tradition of man; it is not Scripture. It began way back in the fourth century after a great persecution toward the Christians was over and Christianity became popular. It came about because the Emperor Constantine adopted Christianity. He greatly encouraged people to become Christians and be baptized and join the church. If any soldier under him was willing to be baptized, he would be rewarded with silver and clothes. Under this condition, who would not be drawn in? They would not only be getting the physical benefit but they also would obtain favor from the emperor. So the church at that time was filled with those people who did not even know the Lord. Therefore, they had to hire someone to be trained to take care of their spiritual needs, and gradually the priest system in the Catholic Church was established.

During the time of Reformation we find even Martin Luther himself preached the universal priesthood of believers, in which all believers should be priests (see I Peter 2:5b), but it was not accepted. It is a common thing that people like to attend the meetings as church-goers and not participate and take responsibility. For this reason, the Protestant Church adopted the Catholic priest system and modified it to become the pastor system. They changed the name for the system, but the function and the responsibility are similar. Thus we have the pastor taking care of everything for us today. People wrongly think, "We do not need to do anything, because if we try to do something we will cause problems." Under these circumstances we would rather not do anything and let the pastor take care of everything. No wonder with this kind of shepherding the body of Christ does not grow. When we exercise oversight, it is true that we need to stand as an example, but do not try to do everything for them. We are to help them, teach them, instruct them, direct them and let them do the things they should do. If we do it in the Lord's way, even though in the beginning it is a slow-moving and difficult task, it is worth it. Oftentimes, we can quickly solve the problem without them, and it is much easier for us to do, but the correct way is to let them go through this process and we go through it with them. The outcome may not be as good as if we had helped them with their problem, but that will allow them to learn. That is the way of exercising oversight.

The Shepherd's Reward

We will conclude with the first book of Peter chapter 5:4: "And when the chief shepherd is manifested he shall receive the unfading crown of glory." Brothers and sisters, those who do shepherding care are not mainly rewarded today. Our main reward is in the future. If we are expecting the whole reward now we will be very disappointed. It does not mean that we do not experience joy now; we do. At the time we see a brother being restored from his poor condition we will be filled with joy. And when a sister is being fed by the Lord or is being led back to the Lord, then we will be delighted to observe her growth. Of course, we rejoice and that is just a small part of our reward. But remember, in reality we will find that there will be more sorrow than joy. Our main reward is not in this present time, but only when the Chief Shepherd is manifested. When the Lord returns, then to those who are faithful, He will reward them with the unfading crown of glory.

The background of the "crown of glory" originates from the Olympic Games in ancient Greece. At the end of each game those victors will be crowned with a flower laurel, but unfortunately those flowery crowns will soon fade away. That glory was just for a moment; that was all. But those who do the work of shepherding faithfully and are willing to suffer for the Lord's sake and for His body's sake, at the appearing of the Chief Shepherd they, as His under-shepherds, will be rewarded with an unfading crown of glory.

In the second letter to Timothy chapter 4:7-8, we find Paul said, "I have combated the good combat, I have finished the race, I have kept the faith. Henceforth the crown of righteousness is laid up for me, which the Lord the righteous Judge, will render to me in that day; but not only to me, but also to all who love his appearing." Hence we can see, if we really look forward to the coming of the Lord, if we really love His appearing, then we will be watching and praying, we will faithfully be walking in the path of righteousness, we will do the will of God, and because of that we will be rewarded with a crown of righteousness.

We also find this crown in the letter to the church in Smyrna in the book of Revelation chapter 2:10: "Fear nothing [of] what thou art about to suffer. Behold, the devil is about to cast of you into prison, that ye may be tried; and ye shall have tribulation ten days. Be thou faithful unto death, and I will give to thee the crown of life." Here we find that those who suffer with Christ will share the glory with Christ and will be rewarded with the crown of life. When God is satisfied, of course, we are satisfied.

Pastoral care is not an easy work. As far as our concept today is concerned, it is not very rewarding. It is very much misunderstood, unappreciated, even criticized and rejected. But it is one of the most essential functions for the body of Christ to be built up. We are called into the function of this pastoral care, whether in a small way or in a large way, so let us look to the Lord that we may be faithful to the end.

Dear heavenly Father, we thank You for giving us this opportunity of considering together this important but neglected theme of shepherding. We pray that what has been shared will be seriously considered and by Your grace will become effectual to us. May we, by Your grace, all be involved in this shepherding care so that at the coming of our Lord Jesus Christ He may have His glorious church as His bride. This we pray in the name of our blessed Lord. Amen.

OTHER TITLES AVAILABLE
From Christian Fellowship Publishers

By Watchman Nee

<u>The Basic Lesson Series</u>
Vol. 1 - A Living Sacrifice
Vol. 2 - The Good Confession
Vol. 3 - Assembling Together
Vol. 4 - Not I, But Christ
Vol. 5 - Do All to the Glory of God
Vol. 6 - Love One Another

Aids to "Revelation"
Amazing Grace
Back to the Cross
A Balanced Christian Life
The Better Covenant
The Body of Christ: A Reality
The Character of God's Workman
Christ the Sum of All Spiritual Things
The Church and the Work – 3 Vols
"Come, Lord Jesus"
The Communion of the Holy Spirit
The Finest of the Wheat – Vol. 1
The Finest of the Wheat – Vol. 2
From Faith to Faith
From Glory to Glory
Full of Grace and Truth – Vol. 1
Full of Grace and Truth – Vol. 2
Gleanings in the Fields of Boaz
The Glory of His Life
God's Plan and the Overcomers
God's Work
Gospel Dialogue
Grace for Grace
Heart to Heart Talks
Interpreting Matthew
Journeying towards the Spiritual
The King and the Kingdom of Heaven
The Latent Power of the Soul
Let Us Pray
The Life That Wins
The Lord My Portion
The Messenger of the Cross
The Ministry of God's Word
My Spiritual Journey
The Mystery of Creation
Powerful According to God
Practical Issues of This Life
The Prayer Ministry of the Church
The Release of the Spirit
Revive Thy Work
The Salvation of the Soul
The Secret of Christian Living
Serve in Spirit
The Spirit of Judgment
The Spirit of the Gospel
The Spirit of Wisdom and Revelation
Spiritual Authority
Spiritual Discernment
Spiritual Exercise
Spiritual Knowledge
The Spiritual Man
Spiritual Reality or Obsession
Take Heed
The Testimony of God
Whom Shall I Send?
The Word of the Cross
Worship God
Ye Search the Scriptures

OTHER TITLES AVAILABLE
From Christian Fellowship Publishers

By Stephen Kaung

The "God Has Spoken" Series
Seeing Christ in the Old Testament, Part One
Seeing Christ in the Old Testament, Part Two
Seeing Christ in the New Testament

Discipled to Christ
God's Purpose for the Family
The Gymnasium of Christ
In the Footsteps of Christ
The Songs of Degrees – *Meditations on Fifteen Psalms*
The Splendor of His Ways – *Seeing the Lord's End in Job*
New Covenant Living & Ministry
Shepherding

ORDER FROM: 11515 Allecingie Parkway Richmond, VA 23235
www.c-f-p.com